Christmas
Blessings

ALSO BY JUNE COTNER

Amazing Graces
Animal Blessings
Baby Blessings
Back to Joy
Bedside Prayers
Bless the Beasts
Bless the Day
Comfort Prayers
Dog Blessings
Family Celebrations
Forever in Love
Garden Blessings
Get Well Wishes
Graces
Gratitude Prayers
Heal Your Soul, Heal the World
The Home Design Handbook
House Blessings
Looking for God in All the Right Places
Miracles of Motherhood
Mothers and Daughters
Pocket Prayers
Say a Little Prayer: A Journal
Serenity Prayers
Soar! Follow Your Dreams
Teen Sunshine Reflections
To Have and To Hold
Toasts
Wedding Blessings
Wishing You Well

Christmas Blessings

Prayers and Poems to Celebrate the Season

June Cotner

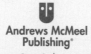

Andrews McMeel Publishing®

Kansas City • Sydney • London

Andrews McMeel Publishing, LLC
an Andrews McMeel Universal company
1130 Walnut Street, Kansas City, Missouri 64106

www.andrewsmcmeel.com

15 16 17 18 19 SDB 10 9 8 7 6 5 4 3 2 1

ISBN: 978-1-4494-7188-0

Library of Congress Control Number: 2015942179

ATTENTION: SCHOOLS AND BUSINESSES
Andrews McMeel books are available at quantity discounts with
bulk purchase for educational, business, or sales promotional use.
For information, please e-mail the Andrews McMeel Publishing
Special Sales Department: specialsales@amuniversal.com.

Christmas Blessings is dedicated
with love and appreciation
to Denise Marcil.

Thanks so much for your
never-wavering belief in this book.

Merry Christmas!

CONTENTS

seven

INSPIRATION 129

LETTER TO READERS

Christmas Blessings grew in my heart long before it became a book. My fondest memories of Christmas include our family traditions of putting treasured ornaments and lights on the tree, decorating our home, and placing special Christmas books on the coffee table. Because I love Christmas so much, I wanted to create a book that celebrates the meaning of Christmas and captures the feelings associated with our most cherished memories and traditions.

When I was a child I loved decorating our tree and attending the candlelight Christmas Eve church service. I loved baking with my mother, singing and listening to Christmas music, and laughing at family gatherings. As the years have passed, my role at Christmas has changed from daughter to mother, and now grandmother. I still have the same warm feelings about this special season. I still love to bake—now with my grandchildren— listen to Christmas music, and sing Christmas carols. Family gatherings are filled with the love and memories of Christmases from my childhood.

Although some may say that Christmas has gotten too commercial, or has lost its meaning, I believe we can keep Christmas alive in our hearts throughout the year by giving to others. We can maintain old traditions and create new ones, we can pause to appreciate the joy in our lives, and we can put life in perspective by remembering the birth of Christ.

In reading this book, my hope is that you will find yourself filled with the spirit of the season. For me, I want to pick up *Christmas Blessings* and be inspired to be kinder, more giving, and more appreciative of everyday blessings. I hope you enjoy this book; it has been such a delight to create!

June Cotner
P.O. Box 2765
Poulsbo, WA 98370
june@junecotner.com
www.junecotner.com

THANKS

My deepest appreciation goes to my agent, Denise Marcil, for believing in *Christmas Blessings* right from the beginning. I appreciate the enthusiastic support of Denise's partner, Anne Marie O'Farrell, at Marcil-O'Farrell Literary.

A special thanks to my longtime editor, Patty Rice, at Andrews McMeel Publishing, for your professionalism, creativity, and wonderful support. It's delightful to have worked with you on a total of ten books now!

Heartfelt love and gratitude go to my family and friends for making every Christmas so special. I am especially grateful to my husband, Jim, for his love and encouragement (and for cooking such a wonderful dinner every Christmas!); my daughter, Kirsten; and my son, Kyle.

Christmas Blessings could not have been created without all the poets who have contributed to my books for years now. Thank you so much for sharing your words and hearts with me. Your poems have survived the careful scrutiny of over three thousand submissions. After I chose my favorite selections, a "test market" panel gave me their feedback on which poems and prayers should be in the book.

A very special thank-you goes to the poets, clergy, and friends who provided a very thorough critique: Kirsten Casey, Cheryl Edmonson, Maureen Tolman Flannery, Reverend Lynn James, Father Paul Keenan, and Arlene Gay Levine.

My sincere gratitude goes to all those in the community who have helped tremendously in the creation and marketing of my books. In particular, thank you to the staff at the Kitsap Regional Library who obtain reference books for me; and Suzanne Droppert, owner of Liberty Bay Books in Poulsbo, Washington, who gives me honest feedback all along the book production stage and enthusiastically recommends my books to other booksellers.

Finally, I thank God, for blessing me with a life full of love, and energy to do the work I love.

one

Christmas Joys

THE SIGHTS AND SOUNDS OF CHRISTMAS

The sound of joyful church bells
Heard from a distant hill,
A warm and cozy fireside
To chase the winter's chill.

The jingle of the sleigh bells,
A Christmas candle's glow,
The cherished celebrations
Each heart has come to know.

A child's anticipation
As he peers beneath the tree,
And finds the gift he asked for
When he sat on Santa's knee.

The sights and sounds of Christmas
Woefully will depart,
But the wondrous love of Jesus
Can remain within each heart.

∽ CATHERINE JANSSEN IRWIN

IF I WERE A CHRISTMAS TREE

I'd
like
to be a
Christmas
tree with pres-
ents all around;
with golden ropes,
and silver
tinsel hanging
to the ground. I'd
trim my boughs with
crystal balls of red and blue
and white, and watch them glow
and catch the gleam of every Christmas
light. I'd wrap myself in
candy canes and popcorn balls,
and such. And, last, I'd have a shining
angel for my crowning touch! Then early
Christmas morn when little ones, with shouts
of joy, rush in to see and claim and treasure every
wondrous toy, I'd lean my boughs to brush up close and
touch each child like this, and place upon each shining cheek my
loving
Christmas
kiss!

— BONNIE COMPTON HANSON

EVERYWHERE CHRISTMAS

Peace on earth—
It's Christmas;
Silent is the night.

All about
the beauty—
Earth is dressed in white.

Listen;
Hear the angels—
Songs are in the air.

Wide eyes
shine in wonder—
It's Christmas everywhere.

◦— JOAN STEPHEN

CHRISTMAS COMES EVERYWHERE

Finns feast on Christmas Eve; salt fish
and potatoes at midnight for the Portuguese,
while Germans like their roast goose on
Christmas Day. Grandfather Frost arrives
with gifts for Russian children on January 7,
while Saint Nicholas delivers to Belgium
boys and girls on December 6. In Norway,
Julenisse, the Christmas elf, gifts all children
on Christmas Eve. Christkindl, a beautiful girl-angel,
comes down from heaven bringing bounty
to some Austrian towns. Santa Claus slides
down our chimneys in scarlet velvet and
soot-stained fur, but arrives Down Under
on water skis, wearing a beard and bathing trunks.
Swedish maidens in candle-lit crowns parade,
paying homage to St. Lucia, while the English
pull crackers, play charades, and attend pantomimes.
Such different ways to celebrate the one purpose
we share—Christmas, the mass of Christ.

~ SUZANNE C. COLE

I HEARD THE BELLS ON CHRISTMAS DAY

From *Christmas Bells*

I heard the bells on Christmas Day
Their old, familiar carols play,
   And wild and sweet
   The words repeat
Of peace on earth, good-will to men!

And thought how, as the day had come
The belfries of all Christendom
   Had rolled along
   The unbroken song
Of peace on earth, good-will to men!

Till, ringing, singing on its way,
The world revolved from night to day
   A voice, a chime,
   A chant sublime
Of peace on earth, good-will to men!

℀ HENRY WADSWORTH LONGFELLOW

PRAYER FOR THE DANCE

May we dance with timbrel, harp,
And thank the Lord above
For blessing us with bounteous gifts,
Emblems of His love.
May we dance with tambourine,
And give Him highest praise,
And leap for joy upon life's stage,
And love Him all our days.

∾ NORMA WOODBRIDGE

THE SOUND OF MY HEART

Wind and rain battle outside.
I've a fire going within, but . . .
It's Christmas Eve
My children are far from home,
And the house is too quiet.

"Don't come," I said. "It's too far.
I'll be fine."
And I am . . . really . . .
Just a bit lonely
For the sound of little feet
And voices raised in song.

Over the crash of the storm
Comes a knock at the door.
In tumble my children and their little ones
Filling my world with love and laughter.

Thankfully they heard not my words,
but my heart.

  — JANICE M. YUWILER

A VISIT FROM ST. NICHOLAS

'Twas the night before Christmas, when all through
    the house
Not a creature was stirring, not even a mouse;
The stockings were hung by the chimney with care,
In hopes that St. Nicholas soon would be there;

The children were nestled all snug in their beds,
While visions of sugar-plums danced through
    their heads;
And Mama in her 'kerchief, and I in my cap,
Had just settled our brains for a long winter's nap,

When out on the lawn there arose such a clatter,
I sprang from my bed to see what was the matter.
Away to the window I flew like a flash,
Tore open the shutters and threw up the sash.

The moon on the breast of the new-fallen snow
Gave a luster of mid-day to objects below,
When, what to my wondering eyes did appear,
But a miniature sleigh, and eight tiny reindeer,

With a little old driver so lively and quick,
I knew in a moment he must be St. Nick.
More rapid than eagles his coursers they came,
And he whistled, and shouted, and he called them
   by name:

"Now Dasher! now, Dancer! now, Prancer
   and Vixen!
On, Comet! on, Cupid! on, Donder and Blitzen!
To the top of the porch! To the top of the wall!
Now dash away! Dash away! Dash away, all!"

As leaves that before the wild hurricane fly,
When they meet with an obstacle, mount to the sky,
So up to the house-top the coursers they flew,
With the sleigh full of toys, and St. Nicholas too—

And then in a twinkling, I heard on the roof
The prancing and pawing of each little hoof.
As I drew in my head, and was turning around,
Down the chimney St. Nicholas came with
   a bound.

He was dressed all in fur, from his head to his foot,
And his clothes were all tarnished with ashes
   and soot;
A bundle of toys he had flung on his back,
And he looked like a peddler just opening his pack.

His eyes—how they twinkled! his dimples:
   how merry!
His cheeks were like roses, his nose like a cherry!
His droll little mouth was drawn up like a bow,
And the beard on his chin was as white as the snow;

The stump of a pipe he held tight in his teeth,
And the smoke it encircled his head like a wreath;
He had a broad face and a round little belly
That shook when he laughed, like a bowl full
   of jelly.

He was chubby and plump, a right jolly old elf,
And I laughed when I saw him in spite of myself;
A wink of his eye and a twist of his head
Soon gave me to know I had nothing to dread;

He spoke not a word, but went straight to his work,
And filled all the stockings; then turned with a jerk,
And laying his finger aside of his nose,
And giving a nod, up the chimney he rose.

He sprang to his sleigh, to his team gave a whistle,
And away they all flew like the down of a thistle.
But I heard him exclaim ere he drove out of sight—

"HAPPY CHRISTMAS TO ALL
AND TO ALL A GOOD NIGHT!"

— CLEMENT C. MOORE

(While Clement C. Moore is widely attributed as the author of
"A Visit from St. Nicholas," there is currently well-documented
research that Henry Livingston Jr. is the actual author of the piece.
For more information, see www.henrylivingston.com.)

THE BELLS

Hear the sledges with the bells,
Silver bells!
What a world of merriment their
melody foretells!
How they tinkle, tinkle, tinkle,
In the icy air of night!
While the stars that oversprinkle
All the heavens seem to twinkle
With a crystalline delight;
Keeping time, time, time,
In a sort of Runic rhyme,
To the tintinnabulation that so
musically wells
From the bells, bells, bells, bells,
Bells, bells, bells—
From the jingling and the
tinkling of the bells.

⌁ EDGAR ALLAN POE

CHRISTMAS EMBERS

The ribbon that ties together
the gift of caring
is both long and wide.
It ties us together
as we share holiday moments
and create homemade memories
by the fires of family love
and special friendship.

It's in the noise of celebration
that we experience joy
and in the serenity of solitude
that we find peace;
So as the year's log
burns slowly down,
recording remembrances
on the parchment
of our hearts,
We can be thankful
to be bound closely together.

Individual gifts, warmly wrapped
by busy hands,
reflect an investment
of time and thought;
but it is the gift of caring
that will most surely
endure.

— TRISH KASPAR

TELL ME AGAIN

Tell me again the story of Christmas,
Sing me the songs a hundred times,
I want to remember the beautiful things,
Heart wonder and tinsel and rhymes,
Trim me a tree and light it with love,
Then Bethlehem won't seem far away
Give me a manger and give me a star,
Then it will be a real Christmas day!

— MARION SCHOEBERLEIN

CHRISTMAS

An azure sky,
All star bestrewn.
A lowly crib,
A hushed room.
An open door,
A hill afar,
Where little lambs
And shepherds are.
To such a world,
On such a night,
Came Jesus—
Little Lord of Light.

⟜ MARY I.

THE JOY OF GIVING

Somehow, not only for Christmas
But all the long year through,
The joy that you give to others
Is the joy that comes back to you;
And the more you spend in blessing
The poor and lonely and sad;
The more of your heart's possessing
Returns to make you glad.

～ JOHN GREENLEAF WHITTIER

two

Through Children's Eyes

FIVE AT CHRISTMAS

Dear God,

    Every year, for at least the twinkle of a star, help me remember what it's like to be five at Christmas. Let me sprinkle oats for the reindeer and bake cookies for Santa. Let me notice every Nativity scene and want more than anything to hold Baby Jesus in *my* arms. Grant me the magic of being awakened by sleigh bells, and being so excited that sleep only comes after three cups of hot chocolate and half of Santa's cookies. Help me remember how hard it is to keep secrets, especially when I have the best present in the world for the one I love the most. And remind me that sometimes the best present is *not* the present, but the box. That's all, God. I just don't want ever to forget how perfectly, specially scrumptious it is to be five at Christmas.

    Amen.

        ⌒ BETTY WILLIAMSON

TO SANTA,

Thank you
for the presents.
Use our bathroom
if you need to.

~ KALI SKILES, AGE 5

YES, VIRGINIA, THERE IS A SANTA CLAUS

I am 8 years old. Some of my little friends say there is no Santa Claus. Papa says, "If you see it in The Sun, *it's so." Please tell me the truth, is there a Santa Claus?*

— *Virginia O'Hanlon*

Virginia, your little friends are wrong. They have been affected by the skepticism of a skeptical age. They do not believe except they see. They think that nothing can be which is not comprehensible by their little minds. All minds, Virginia, whether they be men's or children's are little. In this great universe of ours, man is a mere insect, an ant in his intellect as compared with the boundless world about him, as measured by the intelligence capable of grasping the whole truth and knowledge.

Yes, Virginia, there is a Santa Claus. He exists as certainly as love and generosity and devotion exist, and you know how they abound and give to your life its highest beauty and joy. Alas! how dreary would be the world if there were no Santa Claus! It would be as dreary as if there were no Virginias. There would be no childlike faith then, no poetry, no romance to make tolerable this existence. We should have no enjoyment, except in sense and sight. The eternal light with which childhood fills the world would be extinguished.

Not believe in Santa Claus! You might as well not believe in fairies! You might get your papa to hire men to watch in all the chimneys on Christmas Eve to catch Santa Claus, but even if they did not see Santa Claus coming down, what would that prove? Nobody sees Santa Claus. The most real things in the world are those that neither children nor men can see.

No Santa Claus! Thank God he lives, and he lives forever. A thousand years from now, Virginia, nay ten times ten thousand years from now, he will continue to make glad the hearts of children.

— FRANCIS P. CHURCH
THE NEW YORK SUN, 1897

FOR IT IS GOOD TO BE CHILDREN

For it is good to be children sometimes, and never
better than at Christmas, when its mighty Founder
was a child Himself.

⌒ CHARLES DICKENS

CRADLE HYMN

Away in a manger, no crib for a bed
The little Lord Jesus laid down His sweet head.
The stars in the bright sky looked down where
    He lay—
The little Lord Jesus asleep on the hay.

The cattle are lowing, the baby awakes,
But little Lord Jesus, no crying he makes.
I love thee, Lord Jesus! Look down from the sky,
And stay by my cradle till morning is nigh.

⟿ AUTHOR UNKNOWN

FOR THESE PRECIOUS ONES

Behold, children are a gift of the Lord.
⌐ Psalm 127:3

For plump-cheeked grins
and dancing eyes;
teddy bear hugs
wrapped in footed pajamas;
for the music in giggles
and poetry in pattering feet;
for these small ones who
capture our hearts—
for the gift of children at Christmas . . .
and always . . .
Thank you, Lord.

⌐ EMILY KING

CHILDHOOD MEMORIES

Our hearts grow tender with childhood memories
and love of kindred, and we are better throughout
the year for having, in spirit, become a child again at
Christmas-time.

        ⌒ LAURA INGALLS WILDER

Christmas is sights, especially the sights of Christmas
reflected in the eyes of a child.

        ⌒ WILLIAM SAROYAN

Christmas waves a magic wand over this world, and
behold, everything is softer and more beautiful.

        ⌒ NORMAN VINCENT PEALE

WHAT WILL YOUR
CHILDREN REMEMBER?

Many people nowadays say that Christmas is for
children. . . . Perhaps they have misplaced their sense
of wonder. . . . My memories cover six decades, and
I am again a little child at Christmas.

⌒ FERROL SAMS

What will your children remember about Christmas
Day, when it finally arrives? . . . Years from now, as
adults, they catch a glimpse of something, hear a
snatch of song, smell food cooking . . . and today will
return to them in a flood of memory.

⌒ BISHOP EDMOND LEE BROWNING

Sometimes the smallest family rituals create the
richest memories.

⌒ NICOLE WISE

three

Christmas Angels

ANGELS

Whether angels come rarely
Or are always here,
Whether some have special errands
Chosen or volunteer,
Or are so high in rank
They never appear,
Whether they reflect true light
In their own form clear,
Or manifest as pure
Forces of atmosphere,
Whether earthward Christmas
Or any time of year
I believe, I believe
In what's above, and near.

⌐ IDA FASEL

LOVE CAME DOWN AT CHRISTMAS

Love came down at Christmas,
Love all lovely, love divine;
Love was born at Christmas,
Star and angels gave the sign.

⌒ CHRISTINA ROSSETTI

OF ANGELS

We consider that angels
May be lit from within,
Possess snow-white wings
And speech gleaned from the stars.
But let us also consider
That angels may have
Clothes that need mending.
They may stand at bus stops
Waiting for a ride.
They may have dirty hands
And tired eyes.
Let us consider
The entire realm of angels,
Even as they may exist on Earth.

— CORRINE DE WINTER

WE SHALL FIND PEACE

We shall find peace.
We shall hear the angels.
We shall see the sky sparkling
with diamonds.

— ANTON CHEKHOV

THE ANGEL GABRIEL

And in the sixth month the angel Gabriel was sent from God unto a city of Galilee, named Nazareth, To a virgin espoused to a man whose name was Joseph, of the house of David; and the virgin's name *was* Mary.

And the angel came in unto her, and said, Hail, *thou that art* highly favoured, the Lord *is* with thee: blessed *art* thou among women. And when she saw *him,* she was troubled at his saying, and cast in her mind what manner of salutation this should be.

And the angel said unto her, Fear not, Mary: for thou hast found favour with God. And, behold, thou shalt conceive in thy womb, and bring forth a son, and shalt call his name JESUS.

He shall be great, and shall be called the Son of the Highest: and the Lord God shall give unto him the throne of his father David: And he shall reign over the house of Jacob for ever; and of his kingdom there shall be no end.

Then said Mary unto the angel, How shall this be, seeing I know not a man? And the angel answered and said unto her, The Holy Ghost shall come upon thee, and the power of the Highest shall overshadow thee: therefore also that holy thing which shall be born of thee shall be called the Son of God.

And, behold, thy cousin Elisabeth, she hath also conceived a son in her old age: and this is the sixth month with her, who was called barren. For with God nothing shall be impossible.

⌒ LUKE 1:26–37 (KJV)

GABRIEL

I am Gabriel, trusted Messenger from God.
I have announced, guided, and instructed
God's chosen ones for millennia.

I have always had certitude about my mission.
I remain calm, serene, and easily pick the
    perfect moment.
But tonight I shake and quake and flutter

with the significance of my message
to a handmaiden from Nazareth, a virgin,
not yet twenty years, a lowly handmaid from a
    lowly country.

I must tell her that she will bear the Son of the
    Most High,
that He will reign over the house of Jacob
that His kingdom will have no end.

She will be stunned at my very visit.
She is so humble that she will find it difficult
to believe that she has found favor with God.

How will I ever begin to explain that she will
    be overshadowed
by the Holy Spirit and will bring forth a son,
the perfect Man, the Saviour of all time?

What if I garble the message? What if she says, "No"?
I must stop this pacing, this rehearsing, this jumping
to conclusions. The moment is almost here.

I must resume the grace of my angel ways,
plunge to earth, and face this greatest
moment in my eternal life.
I am Gabriel, trusted Messenger of God.

⌒ DONNA WAHLERT

(On January 12, 1951, Pope Pius XII declared Gabriel to be patron
of those involved in electronic communication, television, telephone,
and telegraph, thus emphasizing Gabriel's function as a messenger.
—Manly P. Hall, *The Blessed Angels*)

AND THE ANGEL SAID UNTO THEM

And she brought forth her firstborn son, and wrapped him in swaddling clothes, and laid him in a manger; because there was no room for them in the inn. And there were in the same country shepherds abiding in the field, keeping watch over their flock by night.

And, lo, the angel of the Lord came upon them, and the glory of the Lord shone round about them: and they were sore afraid. And the angel said unto them, Fear not: for, behold, I bring you good tidings of great joy, which shall be to all people.

For unto you is born this day in the city of David a Saviour, which is Christ the Lord. And this *shall be* a sign unto you; Ye shall find the babe wrapped in swaddling clothes, lying in a manger.

And suddenly there was with the angel a multitude of the heavenly host praising God, and saying, Glory to God in the highest, and on earth peace, good will toward men.

⸺ LUKE 2:7–14 (KJV)

GOOD NEWS FROM HEAVEN

Good news from heaven the angels bring,
Glad tidings to the earth they sing:
To us this day a child is given,
To crown us with the joy of heaven.

⟋ MARTIN LUTHER

ANGELS IN A VAN

It was my first Christmas as a priest. My duties kept me away from home and I was feeling very discouraged about my ministry. As I walked from my residence to the church for Christmas Mass, I felt nothing remotely close to "the Christmas spirit." So lost was I in my downcast feelings, I barely noticed a man and woman in a van parked just a few feet from where I was walking. The passenger-side window of the van rolled down, and a woman's voice said, "Excuse me, Father, Merry Christmas." Half-heartedly, I smiled and said, "Merry Christmas" back. The woman continued, "Father, my husband and I know that you are very discouraged. You are a gifted and talented man, and God has given you many gifts to help his people. You don't appreciate how many gifts you have been given, and how you touch people with what you say and do. You are a gift from God, Father. Merry Christmas." To this day, I do not know who those people were. To my mind, they were Christmas angels sent by God to lift the heart of a young priest on a difficult Christmas Day. They brightened and warmed my heart, as surely as the angels brightened the manger two thousand years before. I know that I shall never forget the gift they gave me.

⟜ FATHER PAUL KEENAN

IT CAME UPON THE MIDNIGHT CLEAR

It came upon the midnight clear,
That glorious song of old,
From the angels bending near the earth,
To touch their harps of gold:
"Peace on earth, good-will to men,
From heaven's all gracious King"
The world in solemn stillness lay
To hear the angels sing.

Still through the cloven skies they come,
With peaceful wings unfurled;
And still their heavenly music floats
O'er all the weary world:
Above its sad and lowly plains
They bend on hovering wing,
And ever o'er its Babel sounds
The blessed angels sing.

⌒ EDMUND H. SEARS

WE TRUST IN PLUMED PROCESSION

We trust, in plumed procession
For such, the Angels go—
Rank after Rank, with even feet—
And Uniforms of Snow.

⌁ EMILY DICKINSON

ANGELS WE HAVE HEARD ON HIGH

Angels we have heard on high
Singing sweetly through the night,
And the mountains in reply
Echoing their brave delight.

Shepherds, why this jubilee?
Why these songs of happy cheer?
What great brightness did you see?
What glad tiding did you hear?

Come to Bethlehem and see
Him whose birth the angels sing;
Come, adore on bended knee
Christ, the Lord, the new-born King.

⌁ FRENCH CAROL
TRANSLATED BY JAMES CHADWICK

THOUGHTS ABOUT ANGELS

Zuzu Bailey: "Look, Daddy! Teacher says every time a bell rings an angel gets his wings."

⟜ FRANCES GOODRICH, ALBERT HACKETT,
AND FRANK CAPRA
FROM IT'S A WONDERFUL LIFE

Happy is the heart that believes in angels.

⟜ KATHRYN SCHEIN

Jesus himself spoke many times of angels. Why shouldn't God have created angels, those great, invisible intelligences full of light? Are we going to doubt their existence simply because we can't see them?

⟜ DOROTHY DONNELLY

At this season, let us be mindful of each other. Let us know the shelter of one another. Let us be the angels we have heard so much about.

⟜ CORRINE DE WINTER

four

Graces, Prayers, and Toasts

GLOW OF THE SEASON

An Advent Lighting Prayer

Lord of this Holiest Season,
> We ask Your blessing for those gathered here
> Tonight as we light these candles of Advent.

As we illuminate this season with the glow of hope,
> Let us remember those who waited in faith
> For a Messiah
> And our own hope of His return.

As we illuminate this season with the glow of peace,
> Let us remember the quiet strength of the Virgin
> And live the message of peace
> Her Son gave the world.

As we illuminate this season with the glow of joy,
> Let us remember the elation of
> The shepherds one Holy Night
> And embrace the joy
> Of sharing this moment with those dearest to us.

As we illuminate this season with the glow of love,
  Let us remember the Child,
  Given in all His tenderness to the world
  As our light through every darkness
  And His simplest commandment:
  Love one another.

As we celebrate this Advent,
  Let the glow of hope, peace, joy, and love
  Illuminate our hearts
  And shine through the world
  Like a candle in the night.

⟿ SHARON HUDNELL

TREE BLESSING

In this season
where the dark
outlasts the light,
the earth is wrapped in sleep
against the cold,

in this Advent season,
time of waiting,
may each of us find ways
to step out of the rush
into the quiet,
to open wide our hearts
in gratitude.

Bless this tree-of-lights,
symbol of all that is ever-green,
faithful & unchanging
as God's love for us.

In this tender season,
rich with memories,
let us remember all of those
who have been lights
along our way,

the loved ones that we hold
forever, in our hearts.

⌒ DEBORAH GORDON COOPER

ADVENT PRAYER

Lord Jesus,
Master of both the light and the darkness, send
   your Holy Spirit upon our preparations
   for Christmas.
We who have so much to do seek quiet spaces to
   hear your voice each day.
We who are anxious over many things look forward
   to your coming among us.
We who are blessed in so many ways long for the
   complete joy of your kingdom.
We whose hearts are heavy seek the joy of
   your presence.
We are your people, walking in darkness, yet
   seeking the light.
To you we say, "Come Lord Jesus!"
Amen.

⌒ MARK NEILSEN

A CHRISTMAS GRACE

We thank Thee, dearest blessed Lord,
For all you've given us to share.
Come, fill our hearts with Christmas love.
Your peace be here and everywhere.
Amen.

⌁ FATHER PAUL KEENAN

A GRACE FOR FAMILY AND FRIENDS

Dear God,
As we gather on this holy night,
May the blessings of Christmas
Be found in each of our lives
throughout the coming year:

Joy,
in the simple things in life,
Peace,
no matter the situation in which we find ourselves,
Mercy,
for those in need,
and Love,
of family, God and friends.
Amen.

— SYLVIA MASI

GRACE FOR A CHRISTMAS CELEBRATION

Candles glow in triumph over winter's dark.
Pine and fir scent the house
With the soft promise of life ever green.
The gifts and games of the season give us pleasure
And the bounty of the table before us
Humbles us with reminders of the richness of
    our lives.
For these blessings,
And for the blessings of family and friends
    gathered here,
We are grateful.
And for this season which we celebrate together,
We are truly thankful.

— PEGGY BIRD

CHRISTMAS EVE GRACE

Oh Giver Of All Gifts, on this Christmas Eve we pray that Your Spirit might infuse our giving with generosity and selflessness, and our receiving with joy and gratitude. We are thankful tonight especially for the gifts of loved ones in our lives, for the gift of remembering past Christmases shared through the years, and for those family and friends who are with us tonight in spirit and memory. We are grateful for the abundant love around this table, which reflects Yours for us: sustaining us, encouraging us, and uniting us, even when we are apart. May we come to understand more fully the gift of Emmanuel, God with us, as we open ourselves to receiving Your Presence through our relationships with one another. In the name of the infant Christ, whose birth brings us hope, Amen.

— THE REVEREND J. LYNN JAMES

CHRISTMAS EVE

Time has sped past as we tried to cram everything
into this one small Advent. Thanks to your energizing
presence, O God, we finished in time to scan tonight's
sky for a star and listen for angel songs. Tonight,
led by You, we greet one another across the manger
where strangers become friends, lost becomes found,
and once-a-year haste becomes homecoming.

⌒ MARGARET ANNE HUFFMAN

A CHRISTMAS PRAYER

Loving Father,
help us remember the birth of Jesus,
that we may share in the song of the angels,
the gladness of the shepherds,
and worship of the wise men.

Close the door of hate
and open the door of love all over the world.
Let kindness come with every gift
and good desires with every greeting.
Deliver us from evil by the blessing
which Christ brings,
and teach us to be merry with clear hearts.

May the Christmas morning
make us happy to be thy children,
and Christmas evening bring us to our beds
with grateful thoughts,
forgiving and forgiven,
for Jesus' sake.
Amen.

⌐ ROBERT LOUIS STEVENSON

SHARE JOY!

May the star that shone in Bethlehem
Brighten our path each day.

May Christ's light of peace and love
Direct us on our way.

And may the joy the angels knew
Be shared by us in all we do.

⌐ THERESA MARY GRASS

BLESSING OF THE HOME

May we fill this place
with kindness to one another,
and with abundant care
for every stranger.
By the gentle light of a star,
guide home all who seek you
on paths of faith, hope, and love.
Then we will join the angels in
proclaiming your praise:
Glory in heaven and peace on earth.
Amen.

~ DAVID PHILLIPPART

A TOAST TO CHRISTMAS PAST

Let's tip a glass to Christmas Past
And times we held so dear,
For now's the time to reminisce
And sip a bit of cheer.
Dwell not on sorrow in our lives
But raise our spirits high;
Though cherished ones may go their way,
Their memories never die.

Give prayer for virtues that we have,
Forget the ones we lack;
Keep our sights on future goals
And failure at our back.
Make a vow to treasured friends
To always keep in touch—
The ones we take for granted
Are the ones that mean so much.

Live our lives as best we can
That peers may one day say:
We left the world a better place
Because we passed this way.

— C. DAVID HAY

GIFTS OF THE SEASON

May the holiday lights
always shine in your hearts,
and the new year's birth
spread joy through the seasons.

Let the fresh, fallen snow
bring warmth to your hearth,
and the jingle of bells
sing music in your ears.

May these gifts and more
throughout this great season
take hold of your spirit
and never let go.

⌒ DAWN M. MUELLER

CHRISTMAS EVE TOAST

On this special holy night,
in the glow of candle light,
with friends and family gathered here,
we raise a glass of Christmas cheer.
May God's presence be born anew,
in all we say and all we do;
and on this Christmas Eve we pray,
Christ's love will live through us each day.

‚ THE REVEREND J. LYNN JAMES

A CHRISTMAS TOAST

To the holly and the ivy,
To the Christmas scent so sweet,
To all those who've gathered here,
You've made this day a treat!

∼ MARY MAUDE DANIELS

A TOAST TO FAMILY AT CHRISTMAS

Outside snowflakes are falling,
There's winter in the air,
But in our house it's cozy
all because we are here.
Let's have a Merry Christmas
and the most wonderful New Year,
as we continue on through life,
with the family we hold dear.

— NOREEN BRAMAN

A TOAST BEFORE OPENING THE PRESENTS

The best present
Of all this holiday
Is the presence
Of all of you!

— BARBARA YOUNGER

AN EVERLASTING BLESSING

From the heart
illumination,
transformation,
the wholeness
of accepting God's love.
From within
we learn to give
of ourselves,
yearning to follow
the divine way.
We remember this day
the birth, the creation
whose spirit and grace
lives in all of us,
an everlasting blessing.

~ CORRINE DE WINTER

A BLESSING FOR OUR FAMILY

From the heart of the holiday
may we be blessed
with the greatest gifts of all—
the warmth of home,
the comfort of family,
and the serenity of Your love.

∽ KATE ROBINSON

CHRISTMAS BENEDICTION

The Lord bless you and keep you
and make His face shine on you and give you peace.
As you remember the Child born in Bethlehem
may you also remember to honor the child in your
  own heart.
May you follow the light of the stars in your dreams
and know that God is with you wherever you go.
Let the hope that was born in a stable
be a sign that God can change the world through
  one small child.
May the spirit of Christmas
warm our hearts all year long.
Grace and peace be with you
in the name of the Father and the Son and the
  Holy Spirit
as it was in the beginning, is now, and will ever be,
world without end.
Amen.

⌒ AUTHOR UNKNOWN

BENEDICTION

Christ has no body on earth now but yours;
yours are the only hands with which he can do
  his work,
yours are the only feet with which he can go about
  the world,
yours are the only eyes through which his compassion
can shine forth upon a troubled world.
Christ has no body on earth now but yours.

    ∽ ST. TERESA OF AVILA

five

Christmas
Memories

ndearing
roam
mas Past
v as home.

The magic of the season
With scent of wax and pine,
The aroma from the kitchen
That beckoned us to dine.

The dancing lights upon the tree
That cast their Yuletide spell,
The joyous song of carolers—
Peace on Earth—Noel!

These treasured scenes of yesteryear—
Could prayers but make them last.
Traditions of the heart live on
In dreams of Christmas Past.

— C. DAVID HAY

THE HEART REMEMBERS

No matter how far one has traveled
Or moved from that long-ago door;
The heart goes back home every Christmas
To the memory of Yuletides before.
There are sounds of the laughter of children—
And friends singing "Silent Night."
The tree in the window is magic
And the snow on the outside pure white.
The tinsel and candles are shining—
Making feelings both sad and sublime
As the heart goes back home every Christmas
To savor the blessings of time.

— JOAN STEPHEN

GRANDFATHER'S CHRISTMAS ROCKING CHAIR

My grandfather loved Christmas
In his rocking chair,
It rocked him back to Bethlehem
And all the glory there—
It creaked with all his memories,
Some happy and some sad,
Mostly he'd rock with happiness,
Thankful to God he had
A family to love him here,
A big, old Christmas tree,
Children laughing all around,
Their favorite place to be.

Now grandfather's old rocking chair
Sits in the house alone,
Because he's gone to celebrate
A Christmas all his own
With Grandmother in heaven
I know he's happy there,
I just hope God has given him
A Christmas rocking chair.

⌒ MARION SCHOEBERLEIN

THE YEAR THE TREE FELL OVER

We spent hours that year,
Setting the tree in the stand,
Stringing the lights,
Looping the beads,
And hanging the ornaments
One by one.
When the children came running
"The tree fell over!"
I thought they were teasing,
But then I saw tears.

We spent hours that year
Setting the tree back in the stand,
Stringing the lights once again,
Untangling and looping the beads,
And hanging, one by one,
The ornaments that had not broken.

And when we were finished,
I decided our tree
Was the most beautiful
Christmas tree I had ever seen,
And that we had each learned a lesson
In fragility and resilience,
And, yes, in the usefulness of
Fishing line at Christmas time.

～ BARBARA YOUNGER

A SOLITARY CHRISTMAS

Winter settled early that year
leaving unpicked pumpkins frozen.

No place to go, I settled for
a solitary Christmas, reading
A Christmas Carol aloud to dancing flames.

Winter peace and beauty gripped the woods.
I spent hours watching ice form intricate
ice lace spread upon field stubble.

Evening pulled a purple blanket over land.
I cooked my festive meal.

Awakened at midnight by a muffled sound,
I stumbled to the door, pulled it open,
tugging hard to free frozen hinges.

A doe stood there head down, exhausted,
eyes wide with terror,
lured by slight warmth of the cabin.
For a moment we were motionless,
then she moved past me on wire-thin legs.

I fed her apples and leftover corn
and she fell asleep before the fire.
Quiet all night, at dawn she moved to the door.
As I opened it she moved to my side like a dog.

She lingered nearby for a week, then disappeared,
having given me her gift of trust for
that one enchanted Christmas eve.

⟜ BARBARA BRENT BROWER

TACK MARKS ON THE MANTELPIECE

Tack marks scarred the mantelpiece
Of that old house I knew—
There where we hung our stockings
When Santa Claus was due.

This memory still comes to me
From oh, so long ago;
Wool stockings on the mantelpiece,
Hung neatly in a row.

And after every holiday,
New tack marks would remain,
Reminding us that Christmas
Would always come again.

That old house is gone now,
But in my memory
Those tack marks are a fixture
That I still plainly see.

⌖ HILDA LACHNEY SANDERSON

A SHUT-IN'S CHRISTMAS

Memories of Christmas past
My greatest comfort today.
Most loved and cherished friends are gone.
Time and illness carried them away.

But, oh, those lovely memories
Of joys we lived each Christmas day,
Now come to my mind in comfort
And I bow my head and pray.

— JOAN LINDEMAN

THE CAROLER'S GIFT

Holding my breath, I open the Christmas
   Cupboard.
My mother's treasures are bundled before me,
waiting to be unwrapped and freed from the
   darkness of their storage place,
yearning to be returned to their various Advent
   stations throughout the house.

I gently unfold the layers of paper and uncover one
   of the tall carolers;
his mouth is drawn in a perfect "Oh. . . ." I smooth
   his mustache and straighten his tie.
I hesitate to set him down, as if I am hanging onto
   the arm of an old family friend.
I saw him first through child's eyes, fascinated by
   the real music glued to his mittens.

I locate his wife; her bonnet is surprisingly
  unwrinkled.
Her mouth has the same formed "Oh . . ." and her
  eyes are bright with holiday wonder.
My mother would hold her and I would carry her
  daughter;
together we would be their voices singing "Oh
  Holy Night."

I close my eyes, letting the memories and the tears
  flow, grateful for her gifts of love,
packed with the other Christmas memories here.
  Lifting the family of Carolers,
we call my daughter over. Laughing she kneels
  down, then leans against my shoulder,
and together we lift the treasures out of the
  darkness.

⌒ THE REVEREND J. LYNN JAMES

CHRISTMAS PHOTO

Every year at Christmas
We sat beneath the tree—
While Father took our picture
Holding presents on our knees.

We still were in our nighties—
Old slippers on our feet.
The hot oatmeal was ready
But we took no time to eat.

Today we look at photos,
Laugh or cry at what we see—
Each with some remembrance
Of those times beside the tree.

      JOAN STEPHEN

AFTER THE DIVORCE, CHRISTMAS

I could not have a Christmas tree that year. December came too soon, only a month after my marriage was rent asunder. I could not hang baubles and garlands while I hung my head in sadness. I baked no cookies, sang no carols, lit no candles.

Everyone understood. "Come enjoy our tree," said the neighbors. "Care for a cookie?" offered my friends. "Don't worry about gifts," said my sisters. "You're the only gift we need." And I healed. Without the tree or the trappings, I found the peace in which to rest. Through these good people, Christ blessed me in my sorrow and gave me back my heart.

— MARTHA K. BAKER

SIMPLE THINGS

When we recall Christmas past,
we usually find that the simplest things—
not the great occasions—
give off the greatest glow of happiness.

— BOB HOPE

six

Christmas
Reflections

LET US REMEMBER

And when we give each other
Christmas gifts in His Name,
Let us remember that He has given to us
The sun and the moon and the stars,
And the earth with its forests and mountains
And oceans—
And all that lives and moves upon them.
He has given us all
Green things and everything that blossoms
and bears fruit—
And all that we quarrel about
And all that we have misused—
And to save us from our own foolishness,
From all our sins,
He came down to earth
And gave us himself.

⌒ SIGRID UNDSET

THE FINEST CHRISTMAS GIFTS

The very finest Christmas gifts are not found below
   the tree;
They are never tied with ribbons, nor are they
   something one can see . . .

Yet among the lights so bright and presents
   wrapped and gay,
They are the finest gifts of all for everyone's
   Christmas day.

It's the sense of love and peace that shines in
   people's hearts,
It's the good will of the season in which each may
   have a part.

∾ VIRGINIA KATHERINE OLIVER

WHO SHINES THE STARS?

Who shines the stars on Christmas night,
so crystal sharp, so diamond bright,
then shares their glitter with generous hand
and sprinkles light on snow-bound land?

Who designed the flakes of snow
arranged to catch the pale moon glow
and light the way for humankind
a loving "welcome home" to find?

Who produced the evergreen tree
adorned with golden filigree
and silver chains and amber lights
to deck the halls this night of nights?

Who warms the hearts on Christmas day
with memories of yesterday,
and a dream that some tomorrow brings
a world at peace for living beings?

The Father sends these gifts of joy
in honor of the blessed boy
who by His birth in humble stall
brought us the greatest gift of all.

➤ WILLIAM MCTAGGART

CHRISTMAS GIFT SUGGESTIONS

To your enemy, forgiveness
To an opponent, tolerance
To a friend, your heart
To a customer, service
To all, charity
To every child, a good example
To yourself, respect

— OREN ARNOLD

BEFORE THE CHRISTMAS DAWN

Just before the Christmas dawn,
When time belongs to me alone,
And all the household's still asleep,
All creatures still in dreamland deep,
I feel within the darkness dense
A special Christmas reverence,
As in the hush that stillness brings,
I almost hear the angels sing,
While in my mind I clearly see
The Christ child stirring peacefully.

⌐ HILDA LACHNEY SANDERSON

THE METEOROLOGY OF LOSS

Every Christmas,
as my mailbox
is snowed in
with cards,
I shovel aside
the expected,
keep looking
for the friends
who don't write;
who've moved, don't
forward their mail,
or stop
sending cards;
somehow become lost.

My husband says
to think of the cards
I do receive:
Kodaks of plum-
cheeked babies,

long, long letters;
to think of the friendships
that last, skein back
through years, fit
like old sweaters.

But I still think
of the friends
that drift away
like snowflakes,
their loss
a wind-
chill factor:
the cast off stitches,
the unwound yarn.

⌒ BARBARA CROOKER

GIFTING BASKETS

I look at the weave of the basket,
And think of the weave of our lives—
The ins and outs, the ups and downs,
The circles of families and friends,
I think of each beginning,
And each and every end.

I see the rhymes and colors,
The entwining of our dreams.
I touch strands of strains and struggles,
All present in every seam.

Told are the honored memories,
In folds of joys and sorrows,
The braids of our lifetime,
To handle and behold.

I touch the emptiness,
Of the center hollow,
Stir the lightness of air,
Knowing it will fill with tomorrow,
The expressions of love and care.

So, I look at the weave of the basket,
And think of the weave of our ties—
The straw that touched our manger,
The reeds that laced our lives.

⌁ ANNIE DOUGHERTY

IN THIS MOMENT

In this place is a peace that we have each been
    longing to find,
Deep,
Down,
Within our hearts,
Souls,
And minds.
This is a place where we are with the ones we
    love most,
Gathered around a table,
Celebrating,
Amidst the red, green, and gold,
The feast laid before us,
And the presents opened just this morning.
We remember the past year,
With its ups,
And its downs.
The first steps of a young one,
And the last of an old.

We remember the God who brought us all here on
this day,
Safe, and sound,
And we remember the memories that make up who
we are.
In this moment,
We are protected from the bitter outside world,
In which hate and fear reside.
In this moment,
We know that each of us is loved and loves.
We know that each of us has the ability to become
a peacemaker.
And in this moment,
we pray for a better world.

⌒ KATE BONACINI, AGE 13

WHAT CAN I GIVE HIM?

What can I give him,
Poor as I am?
If I were a shepherd,
I would bring a lamb,
If I were a wise man,
I would do my part;
Yet what can I give him—
Give him my heart.

— CHRISTINA ROSSETTI

MOMENTS OF JOY

Kids keep you focused on the here and now. That's good, because it forces me to look up and find whatever joy I can muster, rather than allow this dark cloud to overshadow my whole life. I think that's what Christmas will be like this year. There will be moments of sadness, but there also will be moments of joy.

— LISA BEAMER

(Widow of September 11 hero Todd Beamer, passenger onboard Flight 93 that crashed in rural Pennsylvania.)

THE IMPORTANCE OF CHRISTMAS

When nights are at their longest
and the darkest of the year,
the sparkling lights of Christmas
come to change the gloom to cheer.
And just when bones are weary
of the winter winds so cold,
Christmas comes a'calling,
bringing warmth to chilly souls.
When all around is hopeless,
or to us it surely seems,
Christmas gives each child-like heart
new strength to trust in dreams.

⌒ KAREN JOY GANON

IN CHINA DURING CHRISTMAS

In China, there is no Christmas.
There is no recognition of December twenty-fifth.
It is a regular workday, a normal school day.
No one spends weeks selecting just the right gift
    for someone;
no one gives gifts.
You do not tip the mail carrier, the deliverer of
    your newspaper,
the person who, rain or snow, collects your trash.

There are no pine trees shimmering with
    colorful lights,
raining with tinsel, crowned by an angel.
There is no manger scene below it.
The father and mother with child are unknown.
The wise men with exotic names remain
    anonymous—
their presence and their gifts not understood.

There are no gingerbread men baking their spices
    into the kitchen,
no eggnog and rum standing by for a guest who
    may drop in.
There is no Christmas turkey or goose turning
    golden brown.
No carols are heard. No "Silent Night," No "O
    Come All Ye Faithful,"
no "Jingle Bells." In fact, there are no bells.
    Nothing is tinkling,
not even the steady rhythm of the Salvation Army
    bell outside a market.
In China, there are many holidays, but no Christmas.
If your work takes you abroad to live in China
you must pack up an artificial tree and collection
    of ornaments,
your shepherds and sheep and manger figurines.
The recipes for favorite Christmas cookies must
    be collected;
you must slip in a book of carols and the recordings
    that inspire you each year.

In China or someplace else where December
    twenty-fifth is just another day
you must carry Christmas with you.
You must reflect the beauty of the tree,
the love of the family by the manger,
the significance of the carols,
the hospitality of aromatic sweets and the warmth
    of eggnog with rum.
You must unfold the meaning and spirit of
    gift giving.
You must unfold the meaning of Christmas,
elevating it above just another day.

∽ DONNA WAHLERT

ON GOING HOME FOR CHRISTMAS

He little knew the sorrow that was in his
    vacant chair;
He never guessed they'd miss him, or he'd surely
    have been there;
He couldn't see his mother or the lump that filled
    her throat,
Or the tears that started falling as she read his
    hasty note;
And he couldn't see his father sitting sorrowful
    and dumb,
Or he never would have written that he thought he
    couldn't come.
He little knew the gladness that his presence would
    have made,
And the joy it would have given, or he never would
    have stayed.
He didn't know how hungry had the little
    mother grown
Once again to see her baby and to claim him for
    her own.

He didn't guess the meaning of his visit
  Christmas Day
Or he never would have written that he couldn't
  get away.
He couldn't see the fading of the cheeks that once
  were pink,
And the silver in the tresses; and he didn't stop
  to think
How the years are passing swiftly, and next
  Christmas it might be
There would be no home to visit and no mother
  dear to see.
He didn't think about it—I'll not say he didn't care.
He was heedless and forgetful or he'd surely have
  been there.
Are you going home for Christmas? Have you
  written you'll be there?
Going home to kiss the mother and to show her
  that you care?
Going home to greet the father in a way to make
  him glad?

If you're not I hope there'll never come a time
  you'll wish you had.
Just sit down and write a letter—it will make their
  heartstrings hum
With a tune of perfect gladness—if you'll tell them
  that you'll come.

∽ EDGAR A. GUEST

HOME-COMING

For the first time this winter
the designs of heaven have come
fluffing infinite distinctions
down upon the unraked leaves of the pear tree,
the brittle foliage of garden flowers
strawed-over in their dormancy.
Beneath this clean bedding that Advent spreads
I wait for my son's return
from his wandering in the world.
This is the season of coming home.

— MAUREEN TOLMAN FLANNERY

THE CHRISTMAS STAR

It was a very special night
Awaited throughout time;
An extra-ordinary night,
It was my night to shine!

So I shone upon the stable
To lead men great and small;
Wise Kings and lowly shepherds,
I shone down upon them all.

I shone down upon the mother
As she held her newborn son;
I shone down upon the Baby
Who they called the "Chosen One."

But the strangest thing then happened
When next morning I grew dim;
I saw the light was NOT from me,
The light shone out from Him!

I had been but mere reflection
On that great and glorious night,
Of my very own Creator
Whose birth brought all men light.

Yet far from disappointed
No more happy could I be,
Since on that very special night
He shone His light on me.

So when'er you hear the story,
If they tell about my part,
Know the <u>true</u> Star of Christmas
Is the One within your heart!

⌒ KAREN JOY GANON

CHRISTMAS SEASON IN HAIKU

ADVENT
Dark and quiet nights—
Expectancy of a sudden wind,
New star. Wait.

CHRISTMAS
Peace that shakes the world.
One bright flower in the snowfall—
Emmanuel.

EPIPHANY
Magi come and angels
Understand. In the beginning
Is the child.

⌖ LINDA DINI JENKINS

HOLY BIRTH

A magic night
when one bright star,
bending low,

Kissed awake
a tender child
and set the world aglow.

⤜ SHARON HUDNELL

A DECEMBER BIRDSONG

One
silver
birdsong
rings
the Christmas
meadow
and blossoms
my heart
to a rose.

⁓ THELMA J. PALMER

CHRISTMAS WISH

I muse with child-like wonder in the dark
before the creeping dawn erupts with light.
Did I hear a reindeer in the night?
Me, the older one, matriarch,
the grandmother? Of course I did. I still embark
on fancied flights with Santa Claus, delight
in flannel-stocking imagery—a rite
that's lived for years and years within my heart.

An ocean and a continent away
my children's children prance around a tree
with toys and noisy instruments that play
O Tannenbaum in squeaky harmony.
Wakeful in the early dawn, I pray
God bless them all this holy Christmas Day.

⁓ DOROTHY WINSLOW WRIGHT

THE TWELVE DAYS OF CHRISTMAS

From 1558 until 1829, Roman Catholics in England were not permitted to practice their faith openly. Someone during that era wrote "The Twelve Days of Christmas" as a catechism song for young Catholics. It has two levels of meaning: the surface meaning plus a hidden meaning known only to the members of their church. Each element in the carol has a code word for a religious reality that the children could remember.

The partridge in a pear tree was Jesus Christ. In the song, Christ is symbolically presented as a mother partridge who feigns injury to decoy predators from helpless nestlings, much in memory of the expression of Christ's sadness over the fate of Jerusalem: "Jerusalem! Jerusalem! How often would I have sheltered thee under my wings, as a hen does her chicks, but thou wouldst not have it so . . ."

Two turtle doves were the Old and New Testaments.

Three French hens stood for faith, hope, and charity, the three theological virtues.

The four calling birds were the four gospels of Matthew, Mark, Luke, and John.

The five golden rings were the first five books of the Old Testament.

The six geese a-laying stood for the six days of creation.

The seven swans a-swimming represented the seven gifts of the Holy Spirit: Prophesy, Serving, Teaching, Exhortation, Contribution, Leadership, and Mercy.

The eight maids a-milking were the eight beatitudes.

The nine ladies dancing were the nine fruits of the Holy Spirit—Love, Joy, Peace, Patience, Kindness, Goodness, Faithfulness, Gentleness, and Self Control.

The ten lords a-leaping were the ten commandments.

The eleven pipers piping stood for the eleven faithful disciples.

The twelve drummers drumming symbolized the twelve points of belief in the Apostle's Creed.

⌒ AUTHOR UNKNOWN

(Father Hal Stockert is attributed with uncovering this information while researching for an entirely unrelated project that required him to go to the Latin texts of sources pertinent to his research.)

LITTLE GREEN TREE

Isn't it strange how a little green tree
can light up a cold lonely room?
The glow of its light can warm up the night
and melt away sadness and gloom
And the memories that cling to the little green tree
are more precious than tinsel and snow
Of children and toys, of holiday joys,
of Christmases not long ago.

Bring them back, little tree, let me live them again
Let me hear the sweet laughter of friends
Bring it back little tree, all the love that we shared
Fill my heart 'til this loneliness ends.

Now as I gaze at my little green tree,
all the wonders of Christmas seem new
And my little green tree will be waiting with me
until we share our Christmas with you.

⌒ PAT BOONE

WINTER WHITE

Night
and the quiet house
of Christmas-eager children
breathes evenly
as their slumbering energy
is gathered
into deep forest dreams
of the squirrel who sleeps
in the rafters
with his tail
wrapped over his nose,
and outside
the darkness
is everywhere invaded
by specks of cosmic geometry
dusting out the sky,
light
and indefinitely varied
in design
as our aspirations,

falling slowly
like seeds of stars,
turning all the
unfinished business
of fall
into the pure
embroidered
white on white
of a baby's
Christening gown.

⤙ MAUREEN TOLMAN FLANNERY

BLESS THE TREE

Bless the tree,
the one we leave outside;
the tree we trim
with ruby cardinals, sapphire jays
while we stand and watch sunset
plate pinecones into 24-karat tassels
and listen to the wind
flute carols along the fragrant needles.
At the foot, a wreath of walnuts
to entice shy squirrels . . .
their silvery plush
will wrap the trunk in warmth;
at the utmost top
the planet Venus,
a tiny Christmas star
to make this wish on:
Bless The Tree.

— SHEILA FORSYTH

LIVING THE CHRISTMAS SPIRIT

I truly believe that if we keep telling the
Christmas story, singing the Christmas songs,
and living the Christmas spirit, we can bring joy
and happiness and peace to this world.

⌁ NORMAN VINCENT PEALE

WORDS FOR REFLECTION

The best kind of adjectives I use to describe
Christmas, I also use to define my life—simplicity,
values, family, home, and old-fashioned kinds
of things.

    ∽ THOMAS KINKADE

Think about the things you enjoy most in life, and
try to find a way of incorporating them as your own
holiday customs.

    ∽ B. SMITH

There's solace to be found in observing the rituals
of joy when you are alone, afraid, or grieving. To
inhale the scent of pine boughs or light the candles
is to savor a heritage of hope.

    ∽ RONA MAYNARD

This is Christmas; not the tinsel, not the giving and receiving, not even the carols, but the humble heart that receives anew the wondrous gift, the Christ.

⌒ FRANK MCKIBBON

What is Christmas? It is tenderness for the past, courage for the present, hope for the future. It is a fervent wish that every cup may overflow with blessings rich and eternal, and that every path may lead to peace.

⌒ AGNES M. PHARO

My idea of Christmas, whether old-fashioned or modern, is very simple: loving others. Come to think of it, why do we have to wait for Christmas to do that?

⌒ BOB HOPE

Be not forgetful
to entertain strangers
for thereby
some have entertained angels
unawares.

⟿ HEBREWS 13:2 (KJV)

seven

Inspiration

LISTEN TO ME, HEAVEN

Listen to me, heaven,
On this Christmas night,
Put your fingers on the bells,
Your dreams in the starlight,
Make my house a Bethlehem,
Bring the Christ to earth again,
Let the angels sing to me,
"PEACE ON EARTH, GOOD WILL TO MEN!"

Listen to me, heaven,
On this Christmas night,
Put your laughter in the stars,
Make the dark side of heaven light—
Give the world a heart of love,
Shine down with glory on all men,
And on this one night of the year,
Give me a child's faith, wings again!

∽ MARION SCHOEBERLEIN

I KNOW IT'S CHRISTMAS

Yes, God, I know it's Christmas;
I feel it all around,
Not just because of songs I hear
Or snow upon the ground,
I know because my soul is quiet,
Contented and at peace,
As all thoughts born of greed and such
Have suddenly seemed to cease.

I feel a gentle kindness
That is creeping up on me,
And not because of gifts beneath
A lighted Christmas tree.
Yes, God, I'll try to make it last
Throughout the coming year,
While right now I just warm myself
In Christmas love and cheer.

— HILDA LACHNEY SANDERSON

LOVE WAS BORN FOR AN AUDIENCE OF STARS

Long ago
in a tiny, lonely stable
love was born
for an audience of stars.

Infant son
so innocent, yet ageless
bequeathed hope
into seeming poverty.

Could it be
in all our Christmas bustle
we forget
Heaven's miracle that night?

Is there room
in our hearts for those in trouble
finding time
for a homeless child or beast?

If we pause
for an instant in our rushing
stop and think
about good will on the earth

We will find
in the least expected moment
love slips in
giving birth to peace and joy.

⌒ KRIS EDIGER

MAYBE THIS TIME

Let it be this time
that the stable is open
within me.

Let it be this time
that the light is born
within me.

Let it be this time
that Christ is come
within me.

— JOANNA M. WESTON

FOR CHRISTMAS

May you have joy
in the mad rush
of preparation;
may you know peace
in the tiny margins
of time around
the busy days;
may you have star-shine
in clear night skies
for looking at;
may you have silence
now and then;
and, above all—
beyond all else—
may you have love
to give
and to receive.

— ELIZABETH SEARLE LAMB

TRANSCENDENCE

It is Christmas Eve
and my heart has groaned for a season
in great pains of labor
as I tried to birth a Christmas unity
of family spread continent-wide.
Yet this comfort and joy tides me over:

    At an hour agreed
    all will pause
    and gaze as one upon the stars

Remembering the sparkle in loved ones' eyes
Recalling the twinkle of the homeplace tree
Knowing that on this night
The infant, infinite
Son of God has burst into our world
so that we too might transcend
distance and time
through the swaddling spirit and power
of love.

∽ GAIL MCCOIG BLANTON

THE CANDLE

Put a candle in your window
When the night is dark with storm.
It will welcome any stranger;
Keep friends and family warm.

When you see someone in sorrow;
Just let your candle shine
From your soul and from your window
It will be a cheerful sign.

Always place a candle
Where the world can see its light—
The glow will lift a sad heart
And brighten every night.

⌒ JOAN STEPHEN

THE HEART OF CHRISTMAS

May you have the
gladness of Christmas
which is hope;
the spirit of Christmas
which is peace;
the heart of Christmas
which is love.

⌒ ADA V. HENDRICKS

GIFT OF TIME

Take time to laugh, to hug, to cry.
Take time to wish, to dream, to hope.
Take time to wonder, to reflect, to remember.
Take time to talk, to listen, to share.
Time is a gift.
Take time for love this Christmas.

⟿ JUDITH A. LINDBERG

IT IS CHRISTMAS MORNING

As the sun peeks through the early morning frost
And the dawn caresses each flake of snow,
Tiny giggles of laughter alight on the cool, winter
  breeze,
Filling the hallways of every soul with a joyful
  resonance,
Carrying happiness on wings of anticipation, and
Whispering secrets of keepsakes and reminiscence
To the deepest corners of the mind.
It is Christmas morning.
A time for celebration and unbridled excitement,
When all of Creation renews its exuberance for
  peace and love
As children of one world, one universe,
Unite for one single moment in time.
This holiday season may your lives be blessed, your
  hearts be touched,
Your dreams be fulfilled, and your fondest
  memories never forgotten.

∽ HEATHER BERRY

THE JOY OF CHRISTMAS

May the joy of Christmas fill your days with
    gladness
May the peace of Christmas take away your
    anxiety
May the light of Christmas shine through your
    deepest darkness, and
May the love of Him who was born on Christmas
    day go with you in all your ways.

∾ THEODORE FERRIS

THERE'S NOTHING QUITE LIKE CHRISTMAS

There's nothing quite like Christmas
   to set your heart aglow
For every face is beaming
   like roses in the snow.

The beauty of the season
   fills us with delight
And tugs upon our heartstrings
   just singing, "Silent Night."

The weary world is young at heart
   beside a Christmas tree
Where memories remind us
   how good this life can be.

Christmas brings the best of times
   we'll treasure through the years
As we gather with our loved ones
   and remember some with tears.

Hope and faith are born anew
   across the anxious earth
For there's nothing quite like Christmas
   to celebrate Christ's birth!

⟜ CLAY HARRISON

CHRISTMAS ALONE

We're alone for Christmas this year,
My husband and I, our family
too far-flung to gather together.
We thought we might enjoy
not decorating, not shopping,
not wrapping, not cooking.
But we miss the scent of evergreen
and cinnamon, the glitter of tinsel
and gilded ribbons, the warmth of
company, even the clutter, the mess,
and the inevitable disappointments.

So here's what we're going to do.
We'll clean out the attic and closets
and take the good stuff to the shelter.
We'll take long walks and hold hands.

We'll invite the widow next door
to dinner and buy her a little gift.
We'll listen to the neighbor's children
sing carols at the elementary school.
Reaching out to others,
we'll find we're never really alone.

〜 SUZANNE C. COLE

CHRISTMAS CHEER

Put a smile on your face and a good word on the tip of your tongue. Turn on the Christmas music and hum a favorite song all day long. Pour a glass of eggnog and offer it to a friend. Speak kindly to every clerk, cashier, neighbor, family member, and coworker. Then, as you brighten your own little world, you'll make our great big world a happier, gentler, merrier place. And that's good because this old world needs all the holiday cheer it can get—and so do you.

⌒ CRISWELL FREEMAN

WORDS TO INSPIRE

At least for a season, it seems "peace on Earth, goodwill toward men" might be possible after all.

∽ JEFFREY L. SHELER

To want to embrace the world and realize peace on earth is admirable, but starting with the person next to you is truly where universal love begins.

∽ CORRINE DE WINTER

Even if it's a little thing, do something for those who have need of help, something for which you get no pay but the privilege of doing it.

∽ ALBERT SCHWEITZER

If there is love in your heart
Christmas can last forever.

∽ MARION SCHOEBERLEIN

CHRISTMAS WISH LIST

What I wish for you this Christmas won't come in
    a box
or be tied with a ribbon, doesn't arrive by mail or
    cost a cent.
Yet the list is long and sent from my heart
as it opens to yours.
I wish you:
the joy that gratitude bestows,
the splendor of a rose from bud to full bloom,
the energy of authentic passions honored
without concern over worldly success,
the freedom of never judging anyone including
    yourself,
the contentment of knowing yourself as your own
    best friend,
the wisdom to appreciate your mistakes
and forgive the missteps of others,
the compassion required to embrace the world as
    it is
rather than as you would remake it,

the surprising delights of solitude,
the power to let go of regrets as well as anxiety
in order to live gently in the moment,
the vision to see yourself and everyone else
with the eyes of the heart
whose only reality is Love.
Lastly I wish you Light to reveal
these gifts as yours
waiting only to be
unwrapped.

⌒ ARLENE GAY LEVINE

THIS CHRISTMAS

On this Christmas,
may we, the people
of every race, nation, and
religion, learn to love one
another and to forgive
and be forgiven.
Then the peace
of Christ will prevail.

— CORETTA SCOTT KING

CHRISTMAS PRAYER

May the spirit of giving,
Go on through the year,
Bringing love, laughter,
Hope, and good cheer.
Gifts wrapped with charity,
Joy, peace, and grace,
Ribboned with happiness,
A tender embrace.

〜 NORMA WOODBRIDGE

GIVING TO OTHERS

Of course, this is the season to be jolly, but it is also a good time to be thinking about those who aren't.

∽ HELEN VALENTINE

To celebrate the heart of Christmas is to forget ourselves in the service of others.

∽ HENRY C. LINK

Want to keep Christ in Christmas? Feed the hungry, clothe the naked, forgive the guilty, welcome the unwanted, care for the ill, love your enemies, and do unto others as you would have done unto you.

∽ STEVE MARABOLI

Christmas, my child, is love in action. . . . Every time we love, every time we give, it's Christmas.

⌒ DALE EVANS ROGERS

Christmas is most truly Christmas when we celebrate it by giving the light of love to those who need it most.

⌒ RUTH CARTER STAPLETON

A CHRISTMAS WISH

I wish you the joy of Christmas,
The Season's sweet repose,
I wish you the peace of Christmas
To mark the old year's close.
I wish you the hope of Christmas
To cheer you on your way.
And a heart of faith and gladness
To greet each coming day.

⌛ AUTHOR UNKNOWN

AUTHOR INDEX

PERMISSIONS AND
ACKNOWLEDGMENTS

Grateful acknowledgment is made to the authors and publishers for the use of the following material. Every effort has been made to contact original sources. If notified, the publisher will be pleased to rectify an omission in future editions.

Martha K. Baker for "After the Divorce, Christmas."

Heather Berry for "It Is Christmas Morning."

Peggy Bird for "Grace for a Christmas Celebration."

Gail McCoig Blanton for "Transcendence."

Kate Bonacini for "In This Moment."

Pat Boone for "Little Green Tree" by Pat Boone. Copyright by Pat Boone. www.patboone.com

Noreen Braman for "A Toast to Family at Christmas."

SuzAnne C. Cole for "Christmas Alone" and "Christmas Comes Everywhere."

Deborah Gordon Cooper for "Tree Blessing." www.cooperartpoetry.com

Barbara Crooker for "The Meteorology of Loss." www.barbaracrooker.com

Mary Maude Daniels for "A Christmas Toast."

Corinne De Winter for "An Everlasting Blessing," "Of Angels," "Thoughts About Angels," and "Words to Inspire." www.corrinedewinter.com

Annie Dougherty for "Gifting Baskets."

Kris Ediger for "Love Was Born for an Audience of Stars."

Maureen Tolman Flannery for "Home-Coming" and "Winter White."

Sheila Forsyth for "Bless the Tree."

Karen Joy Ganon for "The Christmas Star" and "The Importance of Christmas."

Theresa Mary Grass for "Share Joy!"

Bonnie Compton Hanson for "If I Were a Christmas Tree." www.bonniecomptonhanson.com

Clay Harrison for "There's Nothing Quite Like Christmas."

Harvard University Press for "We Trust in Plumed Procession," an excerpt from poem #126 by Emily Dickinson. Reprinted by permission of the publishers and the Trustees of Amherst College from *The Poems of Emily Dickinson*, Thomas H. Johnson, ed., Cambridge, Mass.: The Belknap Press of Harvard University Press, Copyright ©1951, 1955, 1979 by the President and Fellows of Harvard College.

C. David Hay for "Christmas Past" and "A Toast to Christmas Past."

The Reverend Gary Huffman for "Christmas Eve" by Margaret Anne Huffman.

Robert Irwin for "The Sights and Sounds of Christmas" by Catherine Janssen Irwin. Copyright by Catherine Janssen Irwin.

Jan Jalowski for "The Candle," "Christmas Photo," "Everywhere Christmas," and "The Heart Remembers" by Joan Stephen.

The Reverend J. Lynn James for "The Caroler's Gift," "Christmas Eve Grace," and "Christmas Eve Toast."

Linda Dini Jenkins for "Christmas Season in Haiku."

Anita Jepson-Gilbert for "Angels" by Ida Fasel.

Emily King for "For These Precious Ones." www.emilyking.net

Arlene Gay Levine for "Christmas Wish List." www.arlenegaylevine.com

Judith A. Lindberg for "Gift of Time."

Liturgy Training Publications for "Blessing of the Home" by David Phillippart from *Welcome Yule! 1995*. Copyright ©1994 by the Archdiocese of Chicago: Liturgy Training Publications, 3949 South Racine Ave., Chicago,

IL 60609, 1-800-933-1800. All rights reserved. Used by
permission of Liturgy Training Publications. www.ltp.org

Sylvia Masi for "A Grace for Family and Friends."

Dawn M. Mueller for "Gifts of the Season."

Mark Neilsen for "Advent Prayer" by Mark Neilsen
from *The Lord Is Near* by Mark Neilsen and Henri J.M.
Nouwen. Copyright ©1993 by Creative Communications
for the Parish, Inc. Reprinted by kind permission of Mark
Neilsen.

Virginia Katherine Oliver for "The Finest Christmas
Gifts."

Thelma J. Palmer for "A December Birdsong."

Paul A. Keenan Memorial Foundation for "Angels in a
Van" and "A Christmas Grace" by Father Paul Keenan.
www.fatherpaul.com

Kate Robinson for "A Blessing for Our Family."
www.katerwriter.tripod.com

Hilda Lachney Sanderson for "Before the Christmas
Dawn," "I Know It's Christmas," and "Tack Marks on the
Mantelpiece."

Marion Schoeberlein for "Grandfather's Christmas
Rocking Chair," "Listen to Me, Heaven," "Tell Me
Again," and "Words to Inspire."

Kali Skiles for "To Santa."

Donna Wahlert for "Gabriel" and "In China during Christmas."

Walnut Grove Press for kind permission to reprint "Christmas Cheer" by Criswell Freeman from *The Book of Christmas Wisdom* by Criswell Freeman. Copyright ©1999 Walnut Grove Press.

Joanna M. Weston for "Maybe This Time."

Betty Williamson for "Five at Christmas."

Dorothy Winslow Wright for "Christmas Wish."

Barbara Younger for "A Toast Before Opening the Presents" and "The Year the Tree Fell Over." www.friendfortheride.com

Janice M. Yuwiler for "The Sound of My Heart."

ABOUT THE AUTHOR

June Cotner is the author or editor of thirty-two books, including the best-selling *Graces*, *Bedside Prayers*, and *House Blessings*. Her books altogether have sold nearly one million copies and have been featured in many national publications including *USA Today*, *Better Homes & Gardens*, *Woman's Day*, and *Family Circle*. June has appeared on national television and radio programs.

June's latest love and avocation is giving presentations on "Adopting Prisoner-Trained Shelter Dogs." In 2011, she adopted Indy, a chocolate Lab/Doberman mix (a LabraDobie!), from the Freedom Tails program at Stafford Creek Corrections Center in Aberdeen, Washington. June works with Indy daily to build on the wonderful obedience skills he mastered in the program. She and Indy have appeared on the television shows "AM Northwest" (Portland, OR) and "New Day Northwest" (Seattle).

A graduate of the University of California at Berkeley, June is the mother of two grown children and lives in Poulsbo, Washington, with her husband. Her hobbies include practicing yoga, hiking, and playing with her two grandchildren.

For more information, please visit June's website at www.JuneCotner.com.